From Farm to F

Colleen Hord

rourkeeducationalmedia.com

Scan for Related Titles and Teacher Resources

Teaching Focus:

Blends: cr, gr - Locate words that start with the blend cr and gr. Compare the beginning sounds. What is the same? What is different? List other words that use these blends.

Before Reading:

Building Academic Vocabulary and Background Knowledge

Before reading a book, it is important to set the stage for your child or students by using pre-reading strategies. This will help them develop their vocabulary, increase their reading comprehension, and make connections across the curriculum.

1. *Read the title and look at the cover. Let's make predictions about what this book will be about.*
2. *Take a picture walk by talking about the pictures/photographs in the book. Implant the vocabulary as you take the picture walk. Be sure to talk about the text features such as headings, Table of Contents, glossary, bolded words, captions, charts/ diagrams, or Index.*
3. Have students read the first page of text with you then have students read the remaining text.
4. *Strategy Talk – use to assist students while reading.*
   - *Get your mouth ready*
   - *Look at the picture*
   - *Think...does it make sense*
   - *Think...does it look right*
   - *Think...does it sound right*
   - *Chunk it – by looking for a part you know*
5. *Read it again.*
6. *After reading the book complete the activities below.*

Content Area Vocabulary
Use glossary words in a sentence.
bill
crops
journey
processing plant
restaurant
warehouses

After Reading:

Comprehension and Extension Activity

After reading the book, work on the following questions with your child or students in order to check their level of reading comprehension and content mastery.

1. *What would happen if the farmer did not harvest his crops?* (Inferring)
2. *Why do fresh fruits and vegetables need to get to the stores quickly?* (Summarize)
3. *Have you ever been to a farmer's market? Share that experience with us.* (Text to self connection)
4. *Is it better for the chef to buy from a grocery store or directly from a farmer? Explain.* (Asking questions)

Extension Activity

Draw it out! Using the book, create a picture that shows the step by step process of food from the farm reaching the restaurant. Make sure you show the sequence and label your pictures. Now present your drawing to a classmate, teacher, or parent. Be sure to explain what is happening in each picture. Did they have any questions? Were they surprised with the journey the food took from farm to restaurant?

The food you eat at a **restaurant** travels a long way before it is served to you.

Food begins its **journey** on a farm.

Farmers grow or raise the food we eat.

Some farmers grow fruit or vegetables.
Others raise animals like chickens
or cows.

Foods We Get From Farms

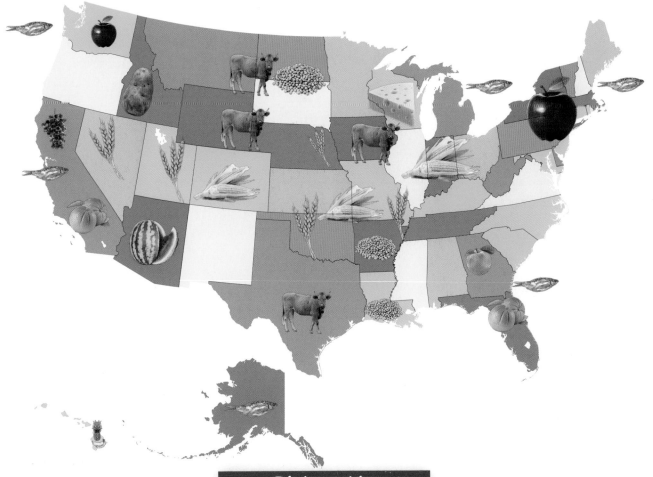

Picture Key

apples   beef   fish   oranges   pineapples   soybeans   wheat

bananas   corn   grapes   peaches   potatoes   watermelons

JOB SHOP

Farmers have to do many things besides growing crops. They repair broken tractors, take care of sick animals, and use computers to keep track of their farm business.

When the **crops** are ready for harvest, the farmer and his helpers gather the crops to sell them.

Some crops, like potatoes, are hauled to **warehouses**.

Crops that must be sold fresh are quickly taken to grocery stores or farmer's markets so they won't spoil.

JOB SHOP

Truck drivers are needed to transport the farmer's crops.

Other food goes to a **processing plant** where it is put into packages.

JOB SHOP

The workers at the processing plant sort, wash, and put the food into packages.

The packaged food is put into trucks
and delivered to stores.

Once the food arrives at the store, the grocery workers put the food on the shelves.

The restaurant's chef shops at the store so he can cook for the people who visit the restaurant.

JOB SHOP

Besides buying from the grocery store, many chefs buy directly from farmers as well. Some farmers deliver their produce to a restaurant.

When you choose what you want from the menu, the waiter tells the chef so your food can be prepared.

After you finish eating, the waiter brings your family a **bill** that shows how much you must pay the restaurant owner for the food you ate.

It takes many people and many jobs to get food from a farm to a restaurant. Perhaps one day you may have a job that is part of the journey.

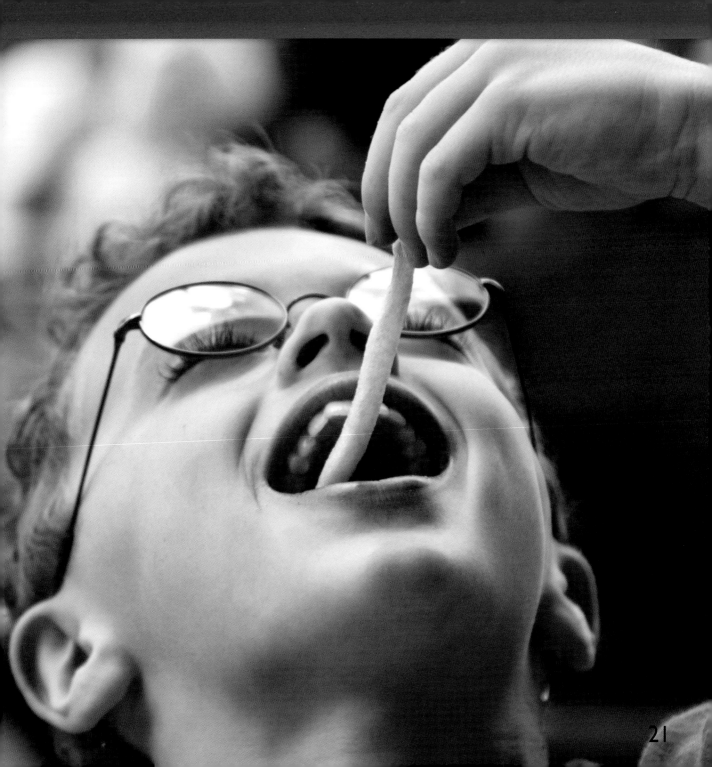

Photo Glossary

 **bill** (BIL): A piece of paper that tells how much money you must pay for something.

 **crops** (CROPS): Plants that are grown in large numbers.

 **journey** (JUR-ney): A long trip.

 **processing plant** (PROH-sess-ing PLANT): A large building where workers do different jobs to get items ready to sell.

 **restaurant** (RESS-tuh-rahnt): A place where people pay to eat meals.

 **warehouses** (WAIR-hous-iz): Large buildings used for storing goods.

Index

Websites to Visit

http://www.fsa.usda.gov/FSA/kidsapp?area=home&subject=ythf&topic=landing
http://kids.usa.gov/jobs/
http://www.nal.usda.gov/educational-resources-children-parents-and-teachers

About the Author

Colleen Hord is an elementary teacher. She lives on six acres with her husband, chickens, ducks and peacocks. Writer's Workshop is her favorite part of her teaching day. When she isn't teaching or writing, she enjoys kayaking, walking on the beach, and gardening.

Meet The Author!
www.meetREMauthors.com

© 2015 Rourke Educational Media

www.rourkeeducationalmedia.com

PHOTO CREDITS: Cover: ©small_frog; cover (middle): ©webphotographeer; title page: ©GoldenPixelsLLC; page 3, 23 (middle): Monkey Business Images; page 4: ©maciejMaksymowicz; page 5: ©visionsi; page 6: ©nullplus22mid; page 7: ©Natasha Tatarian; page 8: ©Peter Irman; page 9: ©elcasanellas; page 10, 23 (bottom): ©Jason Lugo; page 11: ©cogal; page 12: ©tuen van den dries; page 13, 23 (top): ©picsfire; page 14: ©ChameleonsEye; page 15: © DragonImages; page 16: KellyCline; page 17: ©Christian Baitg Schreiweis; page 18: ©Steve Debenport; page 19: ©DNY5922top; page20 (left): ©Ljupcosmokovski; page 20 (right): ©prudkov; page 21: ©Laura Eisenburg; page 22 (bottom): ©Anthony Tiplyashin

Edited by: Luana Mitten
Cover design by: Jen Thomas
Interior design by: Rhea Magaro

Library of Congress PCN Data

From Farm to Restaurant/ Colleen Hord
(Little World Communities and Commerce)
ISBN (hard cover)(alk. paper) 978-1-63430-057-5
ISBN (soft cover) 978-1-63430-087-2
ISBN (e-Book) 978-1-63430-114-5
Library of Congress Control Number: 2014953334
Printed in the United States of America, North Mankato, Minnesota

Also Available as:

ROURKE'S
e-Books